My Opportunity
with God

LAURA MURPHY

WestBow
PRESS
A DIVISION OF THOMAS NELSON

WestBow Press books may be ordered through booksellers or by contacting:

WestBow Press
A Division of Thomas Nelson
1663 Liberty Drive
Bloomington, IN 47403
www.westbowpress.com
1-(866) 928-1240

ISBN: 978-1-4497-2603-4 (sc)
ISBN: 978-1-4497-2604-1 (hc)
ISBN: 978-1-4497-2602-7 (ebk)

Library of Congress Control Number: 2011915517

Printed in the United States of America

WestBow Press rev. date: 10/03/2011

"I dare anyone to read this book and not come away feeling better about the challenges life has thrown at them. It is an incredibly uplifting read."

—William G. Morrissey, M.D.

"I cried, I laughed, it brought the spirit to me!"

—Mary Beth Flynn, R.N.

"This is a must read book, He's yet delivering and working miracles."

—John Jackson, Baptist minister

In simple, direct words, Laura conveys through these vignettes that she provides more than just the sacrament of Holy Communion. She brings warm gifts of kindness, understanding and wisdom.

—Rabbi Edmund Winter,
Chaplain Northwestern Memorial Hospital

"I just loved it!"

—Michael McDermott,
singer/songwriter

"If adversity introduces us to ourselves, then Laura got to know a woman of raw courage and indomitable faith . . . The blessing for the rest of us is that . . . thousands more can now know her too. This is a book brimming with wisdom, grace, and love."

—Laura Palmer, M.D,
Author, *Shrapnel in the Heart*

For everyone.

"Do not see the cross you bear as an obstacle, but as an opportunity."

FOREWORD

Good lives have their own logic, a logic of love. Often, faced with a deadly challenge, those whose lives are ruled by love's logic find themselves unable to escape the harshness of life, unable to protect even themselves or those they love from the ravages of disease or the tragedy of accidents and other losses. Through their love, however, they remain present in hard times to those whom God gives them to love. They make God's love present through their presence. Catholics call the Eucharist the Sacrament of Christ's real presence. The risen Christ is free to be anywhere he wants to be, and he wants to be with us. The Blessed Sacrament is the pre-eminent way in which Christ fulfills his promise to be present to us until he returns in glory, when everyone will finally understand the logic of God's love.

In the meantime, those who bring the Eucharist to the sick bring Christ's loving presence and their own to those who are suffering. Laura Murphy, as a minister of Holy Communion for Holy Name of Jesus Cathedral parish in Chicago, has brought the Eucharist to the sick for some years. In the following pages, she tells us that, "We can all do that." We can all find in visiting those who are suffering an "opportunity with God." Sometimes great tragedy and physical disability leave people embittered; sometimes, however, personal tragedy makes people more available to others, more useful to God. This is the case with Laura, as she explains in this booklet. Her ministry is one of presence, not rational explanation. The logic is that of love. The presence is real and makes a world of difference.

Laura is a realist whose faith tells her what is really important, even when evil visits a person and threatens life itself. Then the faithful realist sees an opportunity with God. What the faithful realist brings to those who are suffering is courage, a courage born of God's presence. What they find in their ministry is happiness, the happiness of being an instrument of God's love for his children and the world his divine Son died to save. In this vision of things, even pain is "valuable," as Laura has the courage to say.

Most of the stories in this book do not have conventional happy endings. Physical death conquers in this life. Resentment kills the spiritual life. Living with permanent handicaps can be a "nightmare," as Laura describes it. What we all have is time. If it is time shared with others, God will bring good out of evil in ways we do not always understand. If our time is hoarded for ourselves, the friendships both new and old that are the opportunity for growth in love will escape us.

I am proud of Laura and grateful that she asked me to write a Foreword for her book. The best thing my cousin's son ever did was ask her to marry him. This is a story of shared life, of new life, because Laura's life bears convincing witness to the logic of love.

Francis Cardinal George, O.M.I.
Archbishop of Chicago

Feast of Sts. Joachim and Anne
July 26, 2011

PREFACE

I survived a serious car crash in October 1987. A few months afterward, Mothers Against Drunk Driving approached me and asked me to do some public speaking for them. It meant a day off physical therapy, a free lunch and some fun times. So . . . of course, I said "YES!"

After I started, I told a friend about some of these speaking engagements, and he said, "You should write those interesting stories down!" At the time, I was only eighteen years old and busy concentrating on other things (like learning how to walk again and getting back to school!) So I ignored his suggestion. Now I am sorry I did. I am sure I have forgotten many remarkable experiences.

Twenty years later, I began volunteering at an area hospital, and meaningful things started happening. Fortunately, I remembered my old friend's advice and this time followed it. Occasionally, I would make a few notes about my day and the patients I met.

As time went on, I noticed many similarities in my stories and the things the patients and I discussed. I thought to myself, "Wait! If all these people feel the same way, there has to be more out there! And what if they don't have someone to talk to?"

So I put some of these stories together. I thought that people might give this small book, instead of candy or flowers, to those they care about who are going through difficult times. Moreover, they might like to read it themselves!

I would like to thank the people who inspired me to write this book—those both in and out of the hospital. We have all experienced pain, and I am sure there is even more in our futures. I hope these stories help you believe we can all overcome hardships.

In addition, I hope this book encourages more people to get involved in similar programs. These days, I think we set the "goodness bar" too high. What I mean is, too often people do not do good things simply because they do not consider themselves "good" enough.

Well, here's a news flash: you really don't have to be <u>that</u> good! You just have to be kind! Only a small number of people can be exactly what they want merely because they feel like it. However, anyone can be <u>kind</u>. Isn't that exciting?

I hope you get as much out of this book as I have.

Peace be with you.

The downtown Chicago crowd nestled into their pews when the priest finished the Gospel. We all sat in silence and waited for some inspiring words. However, I must admit, I instead thought about where my husband and I would go for brunch, the sale at the shops on Michigan Avenue, and all the things I had to do for the rest of the day.

Unfortunately for me, the pew we sat in was not our "regular spot." The many church-goers that day, along with our own late arrival, set us back a few more rows than usual. This relocation caused me to squint as a bright morning summer sun shone through a stained glass window.

"Damn tourists," I thought to myself.

My contemplation about the day ahead, along with this slight irritation, seemed to put me into another world. However, Father Dan then said something that instantly pulled me home:

Do not see the cross you bear as an obstacle, but as an opportunity.

"That's it!" I thought, "I know he's talking to me, and I know what I should do." And so began my work at a local hospital as a minister of care—the ministry of volunteers who visit Catholics and bring them Holy Communion.

ME

I suppose I should begin by telling you a little about myself. I spent four years at a suburban high school on the southwest side of Chicago and really loved it. I was involved in student council, a spring musical, pom-poms, the honor society . . . it was all a lot of fun! However, when graduation came I was ready to move on—to bigger and better things!

That fall, I went away to the business school at the University of Illinois in Champaign/Urbana. It was a great time—I really lived it up! With wild parties and dances, I thought I had it all and that nothing could take it away. However, I was wrong.

I came home one Friday afternoon for my former high school's homecoming football game. Unfortunately, that evening I never made it to the game, and that night I was never coming home.

Just a few miles from my house, while I rode in a car driven by my college roommate, a drunk driver struck us head-on. Upon impact, my face crashed through the front windshield. My head hit the car in front of us, I fell back inside, and I landed on my friend's lap. Thousands of tiny pieces of glass cut into my face, the broken window tore my left eyelid off, the right side of my body was paralyzed, the blow knocked me unconscious, and I immediately started going into convulsions.

My parents arrived at the hospital and found a priest standing over my head giving me the Last Rites. When they asked the nurse if I was alive, she quietly responded, "She has a pulse." Later my friends arrived, and the nurse had to point me out to them because my face was so badly torn up they could not even recognize their longtime childhood friend.

When I first woke up after a ten-day coma, I thought I was just dreaming. I would tell my doctors and nurses not to worry! I was sure I was going to awaken and everything would be fine. I soon realized I would never wake up from this nightmare.

The college life of parties, sports events and study groups quickly morphed into a month at Loyola Hospital in Maywood, Illinois, and three months in the Rehabilitation Institute of Chicago. A year of outpatient rehabilitation therapy followed. There I learned to walk, talk and write again. Although the therapists were nice, the work was hard and tearfully painful. Tasks as simple as fitting a ring on a peg or tying my own shoes were frustrating and sometimes even impossible. I was an eighteen-year-old college student who graduated high school in the top of her class, but now I could not even write my own name.

After rehab, I returned to college. Although I graduated in four and a half years, the effort of college life was not just backbreaking—it was heartbreaking as well. It meant reading a page in a book repeatedly because I would forget the top by the time my eyes reached the bottom. It meant tape recording all of my lectures and typing up the notes later in my dorm room. It meant leaving my room a half hour early to walk to a class that was just across the street. And it meant hearing the people behind me laugh and crack jokes about the way I walked—accusing ME of being drunk! What a paradox! My spastic gait is indeed because of alcohol, but I did not drink it.

The crash also took a large part of my memory. From two and one half years before until one month after the crash are gone, and my mind is only cloudy concerning the events surrounding it. Many describe high school as "some of the best years of your life," and these were the years ripped away from my memory. There were no more football games on a Friday nights—only lonely pom-poms sitting in the corner of the basement. There was no more senior class prom in a long black limo—only a pink, formal dress hanging in my closet. There was no more high school graduation to mark the beginning of my future—only pictures placed solemnly over my hospital bed. There were no more memories—just these empty symbols of a past I no longer had—a past that screamed at me "remember happier times!" And short-term memory problems cause me to lose more precious moments every day.

During the next fourteen years, I met and married a wonderful man, moved to downtown Chicago, and worked different jobs for the State of Illinois. Although I tried to live a "normal" life, my many handicaps triggered recurring problems resulting in return visits to the hospital and more physical therapy. These troubles made it necessary for me to leave my job.

I worried my new life of unemployment would turn me into an overweight, lazy, "couch potato." So I began a light workout routine at a nearby gym. Although my hips were shrinking,

I became nervous my mind would, too! I knew the long days alone at home were mentally unhealthy. They could certainly turn anyone's mind to mush.

Fortunately, that bright Sunday morning at church my squinting eyes saw things clearly. I instantly heard Father Dan's message of opportunity.

* * *

The following are a few people I have met as a minister of care. Although their names are changed for their own privacy, I assure you the experiences I write about are very real. As you might notice, the first letter of the main characters' names together spell out this book's special title phrase. It starts with my own story, "**Me**," and ends with a message to "**You**." This reminds us that we all experience pain.

CHARACTER	MESSAGE
Me	introduces author
Yolanda	hard work is crucial
Oscar	interaction is vital
Patricia	we all have flaws
Peter	pain is valuable
Olga	love is logical
Rosie	good nurses are essential
Terry	presence is a gift
Udant	mistakes are necessary
Nathan	victims go beyond the bed
Irving	God is a giver not a taker
Tina	forgive and forget differ
You	we are never alone

YOLANDA

I first met Yolanda in October. After I peeked my head into her hospital room, I asked, "Yolanda?" she immediately corrected me and said, "My friends call me 'Yo-Yo.'" This fun-loving, single woman in her mid-forties had also been in a serious car crash. Her main injuries included several severe back injuries.

Soon I understood the implication of this silly nickname and realized why it was a perfect fit! I always looked forward to the fun times I spent with her. Although I usually had a long list of patients to see, I always saved her visit for the end so I would not have to rush away. Yo-Yo and I joked about some of the hospital staff, shared make-up tips and laughed about old boyfriends. We talked as if we were teenagers at a slumber party!

One day when I visited Yolanda, a nurse came in. "Oh, I didn't realize you had a visitor," she said.

Yo-Yo introduced me by saying, "This is my best friend, Laura."

<u>Best</u> friend? Hmmm . . . I always thought a <u>best</u> friend was someone you knew since childhood, someone who was close to your family, and someone you gossiped with for hours on the telephone. In contrast, I had only known this young woman for a short time, I only briefly met her brother-in-law once, and I only spent a few mornings talking with her.

However, if you define this term as someone you laugh with, someone you rely on and someone who can relate to your own suffering, then I guess at the time I <u>was</u> Yolanda's best friend . . . and she was mine.

Her recovery started with several days in the regular hospital. Then doctors shipped her off a few buildings away to the rehabilitation center. There she spent long hours in physical and occupational therapy re-learning simple skills many of us take for granted. I often visited her.

"You were right, Laur, this is tough!" She told me one afternoon when I stopped by. "People from the 'outside world' always tell me they can't believe all I've gone through and all I've done. But the way I see it—I have no choice!"

I agreed by saying, "You're right, Yo. My parents brought me up on the idea that hard work is not an option—but an expectation. Anyone would agree our situations are unfair but, as you say, we have no choice! I don't believe God <u>did</u> this to us, but I am convinced He will help us through it." She nodded vigorously with unquestionable but acquired agreement. Her strong accord confirmed what every patient knows. However, in difficult times we all need to be reminded of these truths. The message is "the Word of Our

Lord"—pastors, ministers and rabbis are simply the messengers.

Almost a year later, I noticed her name again on the patient list. This time she was up in the intensive care unit. I rushed to see her and found her barely awake. Nurses informed me she just spent fourteen hours in surgery.

It had been a long time since we last saw each other, so I was not sure she would remember me. Furthermore, I did not know if she would be very alert in view of all of the medication she had received. Yet, as I walked quietly into the room, she turned her head and smiled.

I asked, "Yo-Yo? Do you know who I am? I'm Laura, from the Catholic Church."

She rolled her eyes and softly said sarcastically with a smirk on her face, "I <u>know</u> who you are!"

Although her voice was not much more than a whisper, I pulled a chair up next to her bed, took her hand and asked, "What are you doing back here?! I know . . . you missed me too much, and you had to see me!" She quietly laughed and told me about the difficult decision she made to return for more back surgery. At the time we talked, it was unknown by her doctors if all she just went through would help in the end. Some family members disagreed with her decision to have the operation. The pain she then felt also made her question her choice.

With closed and teary eyes, she put her hand on her chest and whispered, "It hurts right here! Make it stop!" I thought of my own painful experiences in numerous hospitals. Many times, I also begged people to take the pain away. Although I always knew they wanted to, I also knew my pleas were unreasonable.

Pulling my chair even closer, I whispered back, "Oh Yo! I wish I could!" I reminded her, "You've beaten this pain before and you <u>know</u> you can do it again. You just have to wait for your pain medicine to kick in."

A few minutes passed, and as we sat in silence, the lines on her face softened and her grip became more relaxed. I could tell the magic potion in her I.V. bag was doing its work. With her eyes still closed, her tense lips smoothed out across her face. She thanked me for holding her hand and asked me not to leave until she fell asleep.

*   *   *

When I first volunteered for this program, I was not quite sure I could do it. Although I was raised Irish Catholic, with a strong belief in God, I questioned if that was enough. I always attended public schools, I could not quote many lines from the Bible, nor did I always know exactly which saint to pray to for specific illnesses.

Yet sitting there that afternoon with Yolanda, I realized that when a person is suffering often all they need is someone to sit with them in silence and hold their hand. We can all do that.

OSCAR

It was only about 9:30 in the morning. Walking into the dark room, I was uncertain if the stroke patient I went to visit was awake. However, as I drew near I noticed Oscar's eyes were open. I said, "Hello!" and I asked him if he wanted to receive Communion. He gave me a funny look and informed me three other ministers of communion had already been there that morning.

I was fairly sure I was the first minister there that Thursday. However, I did not question him. My own experiences taught me if a person is alone in a dark hospital room for a long time, the days and nights seem to blur together.

The brief talk we already had was full of his slurred speech and included the repetition of phrases. This hinted he was probably a little confused and heavily medicated. "Oh boy," I thought, "this is gonna be tough!" However, I figured this lonely man just needed some human interaction. So, I moved toward the bed and said, "Hmmm . . . Well, how 'bout if we just talk for a while?"

A shrug of his shoulders seemed to ask, "Why would you want to talk to me?" He softly murmured, "O.K, if you want to."

We first talked about our families. He told me he only had one son who did not come to see him often. As far as his friends went, they all lived in the suburbs and rarely made it to the hospital. "I never have any visitors," he concluded, as his sad eyes dropped down.

"Hey! You've got me today!" I reminded him with a light tap on his arm and a grin on my face. He smiled as he raised his eyes.

I sat with him for about a half hour. Our conversation included talk about classic movies and those much-loved old Hollywood stars. We laughed at hospital food and compared our favorite restaurants. When he heard I had been in a car crash and went through a long rehabilitation process, he asked, "Oh, is that when you found God?"

With a smile, I explained that I always knew He was there. Now that I think about it, I guess maybe that is when <u>He</u> found <u>me</u>.

Then Oscar asked, "Why are you so happy?"

"<u>WHY</u>?" I asked. "Did you see the movie, *The Pursuit of Happyness?* It's a true story about that successful stockbroker, Chris Gardner, played by the actor Will Smith? Well, as the character points out, there is no 'Y' in 'happiness.' So, I guess that means it doesn't need a reason! We don't have to explain <u>why</u> . . . it can just be." Then I pointed out, "Smiling is one of the easiest things to do, and it makes you and everyone around you feel better! So, I think we should all do it as much as we can!"

Before I left, I took his hand and asked him to say a prayer with me. We recited the *Our Father.* Just as I presumed, his broken-down brain remembered this well-known prayer that many of us learn in childhood. His face beamed with a proud look of satisfaction after we finished. My own unfortunate familiarity with head injury taught me that successfully completing any task (regardless of its difficulty!) would strengthen his self-esteem.

When the time came for me to move on, Oscar was definitely more quick-witted and on the ball. Without a doubt, his communication skills had improved. A bright glow of energy replaced a once gloomy look of confusion. I promised my new friend I would visit him the next time I was in the hospital.

I returned a few days later. Although I knew what floor he had been on, I could not remember his last name or his room's number. The nurses I asked could not seem to help. I did not know if he went to his home, a nursing home, or if he passed away.

*   *   *

Although my parish sponsors this program and its main purpose is to bring Holy Communion to the sick, I see it as much more. To me, the communion host is just the way to get me in the door. It is my excuse for being there. Like any good host, it makes me feel welcome as I enter the room. However, I feel my real purpose is to make people like Oscar smile before they leave . . . wherever they go.

PATRICIA

An older woman with a pleasant smile occupied the next room. I sat down and noticed many pictures taped next to her bed. They were simple drawings done with crayons, above straightforward messages such as "We love you Grandma!" and "Get well soon!" The ruffled nightgown she wore along with her soft, gray hair reminded me of just about every adorable grandmother character from any primetime T.V. show.

We began our small talk about such trivial things as the unpredictable Chicago weather and the upcoming summer festivals. She told me about her three grandchildren and motioned to their photographs on the small table next to her bed.

I did not know what sickness or injury brought Patricia to the hospital. However, she had many dark blue stitches up and down her face and a few shiny staples above her eyebrows. She worried her new "Frankenstein face" would frighten her grandchildren's young hearts.

I told her about the time I first went home from the hospital. My young nephew sat on my lap and saw the scars on my face up close for the first time. Without anyone saying anything, he reached up, ran his finger down the longest mark and gently kissed it.

"Your grandchildren will know who you are, and their only fear will be that you are in pain. Children simply reflect our own emotions. If you can find peace with your injuries, they will, too. Just reassure them you are O.K. and remind them you love them."

Then I went on, "Everyone has some kind of handicap—some people are rude, others are dishonest and a few people (like us!) have funny marks on their faces. I guess that just means our faults are more obvious. Is that really so much worse?" I laughed.

The discussion continued, and she informed me where her two sons had attended college. "Oh, my husband went there!" I revealed.

"You're married?!" She asked with a puzzled look on her face.

"Yes," I laughed, "did you think I was too ugly to be married?!"

"No, too spiritual!" She continued, "The way I look at it, either you like to, ya know, dance and stuff or else you're spiritual!" (That attitude seems common today and I think that is a shame. Don't we say we "celebrate" Mass? And isn't dancing just another way to celebrate?)

Before I moved on, I remembered why I was there and offered her Communion. She decided to receive it. I first said the long prayer *The Memorare*. She kept very still with closed eyes and folded hands. This, along with the tranquility found in this quiet weekday morning, added to the prayer's spiritual aura.

After I finished, Patricia remained motionless. I figured she was praying, so I did not interrupt. A few minutes passed. I held up the host and said the usual pre-communion "shpeel." Upon hearing this familiar prayer, I expected her eyes to open. But nope—no response.

Bearing in mind where I was, I began to worry. Looking for signs of life, I tried to watch her chest. If it moved up and down, I assumed I could just move on without concern. However, I was unsure of what I saw.

Frantically, I rushed out of the room to the nearest nurses' station. I explained what happened and expressed my concern to the first nurse I saw. She gave me a friendly smile to calm me down and told me she would check it out.

I waited outside the hospital room, afraid of what she would find. Soon, she came out chuckling. "I don't know what you did to her, but she is out cold!"

*   *   *

I wish I could take credit for Patricia's siesta by saying there was some spiritual meaning behind it. Perhaps I could say my presence brought her a kind of divine peace? Or how about if I said the grace of God was sent to her through me?

However, the fact is I cannot. It can often be crazy in a hospital. There are lots of tests and all those status calls in the middle of the night—to check your heart rate, blood pressure and temperature. I realize how vital these tests are, but they often keep you from getting a good night's sleep!

That morning, I think Patricia's body was just answering its own status call!

PETER

"What time is your dad coming?" I asked as I entered the room.

"I'm not sure he's in Chicago," Peter answered nervously as his eyes moved quickly from side to side.

"Yes, he is! The nurses told me he was here yesterday!" I reminded him.

"SSsshh . . . !" he ordered as he waved me close to share a secret. In a whisper, he informed me, "<u>THEY</u> don't know he's here."

"Who?"

"The Russians! They attacked him last night…" Then we heard some racket out in the hallway. "What's that noise?!" he asked suspiciously.

"Oh, it's okay. It's just the nurses' station. Here, I'll close this." I walked over to the sliding glass door and pulled it shut. The silence calmed him down. "Don't worry," I whispered into his ear, "I won't tell anyone where your dad is."

He sighed in relief and thanked me. To this day, my family still teases me about the silly and unjustifiable comments I made during my last hospital stay. I knew the strong drugs given to Peter were driving these anxious remarks out of his mouth.

Then he asked, "How do <u>you</u> deal with the pain?"

The fact that I was in a car crash had not been brought up, nor had I mentioned the extent of my injuries or my lengthy hospital stay. However, I suppose my apparent handicaps suggested some amount of pain was involved!

I explained why I think pain is valuable. Of course being in pain is not, but the ability to feel pain is a blessing. It is simply the body's way of telling you something is wrong. It might be indicating there is a door closed on your finger, a virus living in your stomach, or merely suggesting the love of your life just walked out the door.

When I was in the rehabilitation hospital, I became good friends with a young man down the hall named John. This young man survived a serious car accident that left him paralyzed from the neck down. While there, he developed a sore on the back of his leg. John could not feel it nor turn to see it. Due to this fact, it went untreated for days. By the time the nurse spotted it, the sore was infected. If John had felt some discomfort, the problem could have been taken care of sooner. He might have avoided a lot of trouble.

Therefore, I believe the best way to deal with any pain is to determine what it is telling you and take it from there. This will not always make the pain go away, but it will make it easier to handle. You can then talk yourself through the problem using common sense, as if you were trying to pacify a screaming child. Many say, "What you don't know won't hurt you!" but I say, "What you don't understand will!"

While standing at Peter's bedside, I noticed many dark bruises up and down the inside of his weak arms. Clearly, these represented cries his body made when the technicians tried repeatedly to draw samples of blood. The sight of these "purple pinholes" made me cringe. They reminded me of many similar marks once left on me.

He noticed me looking at his arms and began explaining what caused the marks. I giggled and told him I knew precisely what they were. We then shared our own horror stories about being poked too often and laughed at the idea of there not being any more blood left—our explanation was that the nurses had taken it all!

We continued our talk, and he asked me if I was able to drive. I explained I could not because my head injury caused constant double vision. When he heard this, he grabbed my arm, smiled and shouted in excitement, "I have double vision, too!"

His enthusiastic response made me smile. It reminded me of two grade school students at the park who just learned their puppies had the same name! In the past, people reacted much differently to this news. A pouty lip, sad eyes and a quiet apology was the usual response. However, in this case a pleasant grin came in place of tears.

We immediately seemed like old friends! Both of us could directly relate to the difficulties caused by this shared obstacle. We laughed about pouring spoons of sugar into cups of coffee that were not there and buying "triple A" batteries when we meant to buy "double A."

* * *

This short encounter with Peter reminded me that loneliness is more than just physical.

It is the emotional state of feeling alone and misunderstood. I learned that even if someone is not like everyone, we can be sure everyone is like someone.

OLGA

White sheets lay on top of the tiny couch under the window. A worn out pillow not much longer than the "bed" itself sat at one end, and numerous prayer books and rosary beads crowded the other. Closed blinds covered the only window. This kept out the bright sun light as well as any signs of life hurrying along the busy city streets.

A frail woman with dark hair stood over her husband as he rested in the bed. He was very thin and unresponsive. Although it was obvious the patient could not receive Communion, I introduced myself and offered Communion to the woman. She became excited, gave me a big smile and proclaimed in a Hispanic accent, "Oh, yes! I love to receive Jesus!"

I continued to visit her various mornings. Each time I learned more about her and her husband. They were both immigrants and had little family in this country. Therefore, they did not get many visitors. He had been in and out of hospitals for many years needing several different operations. During these times, she remained by his side, set up camp as she had here, and found a small number of friends in the hospital staff. These few dear employees were often her only source of much-needed support.

One morning while we talked, she suddenly stopped and tears swelled up in her eyes. Worried had I said something wrong, I asked, "Olga, why are you crying?" (Taking into account where we were and why we were there, I immediately realized this question was incredibly stupid!) She raised her hand, motioned toward the bed, shrugged her shoulders and softly said, "He's all I have."

*   *   *

The tiny hospital room had its own bathroom. She used it daily to shower and dress. Most of her meals were made up of leftover hospital food barely touched by her husband. She slept each night on her cozy hospital couch. This allowed her to get a small collection of short naps between late night nurses' visits. After having to spend so much time in hospitals myself, the thought of living here by choice seemed illogical. Thank you, Olga, for teaching me about the logic of love.

A few days ago, I received a telephone call. The voice on the other end asked if I knew who it was. I recognized Olga's voice immediately and asked about her and her husband. In a soft voice, she told me he had passed away.

"It was in the middle of the night and I wasn't there," she informed me. "I really wish I had been there to hold his hand!"

I told her about one night when I was alone in the hospital . . . a bad reaction to some medication caused me to see black spots and I heard a high-pitched buzzing noise in my ears. In addition, the entire left side of my body went numb and I felt as though my lips were swelling. Even though many say "a watched pot never boils" I glanced at the clock on the wall every few seconds. It looked as though the hands were moving in slow motion!

This went on for an entire hour. Needless to say, I was terrified! I laid there frozen. In my mind, I imagined I was in my husband's arms and we were sitting quietly on our couch at home. As far as I am concerned, he <u>was</u> in my hospital room and helped me through an extremely tough night.

*　*　*

"In the same way I held onto my husband during that awful time, I am sure your husband held onto your hand! And your heart should hold onto the idea your husband's death was not God's way to end his life; it was God's way to end his pain."

"Do you think he's in heaven now?" she asked.

"Yes, I do. And take comfort in knowing just as you watched over him for so long, now he's watching over you."

ROSIE

My weak and once-injured legs ached with fatigue. Although I was done for the day, I decided to hang around for a while and sit in a comfortable padded chair in the hallway. In fact, I was sure I heard it call my name! When I thought about the long walk home, my body moaned! I sipped on a warm drink and tried to relax.

In a room not far from me, I heard a nurse as she woke a patient. I could not see them. However, the conversation, along with the nurse's high-volume speech, implied this was an elderly female patient. The energetic wakeup call was refreshing to hear amid these generally somber walls.

"Okay, Rosie . . . Your son is coming to visit today! He'll be here in about an hour!" she reported. "I know you hate that drab, thin, hospital gown, but we'll fix you up! Let me just brush your hair for you . . . here ya go . . . did they wash it for you last night? Now, we'll put some blush on those cute cheeks . . . and a bit of your lipstick (Oh, what a pretty color!) . . . there you are . . . you look beautiful!"

Then in a cheerful voice I heard her remind the patient of some of the plans for the rest of the morning: "Now . . . The doctor will be here soon. All the tests from yesterday look good! You only have one more this afternoon—and it's an easy one! It should be no problem! I'll come by again after breakfast."

I saw a young woman leave the patient's room. Although I had not met her before, I rushed down the hall after her. "Excuse me?" I called. She stopped and turned. I asked, "Are you that patient's nurse?"

"Yes?" she responded with a pleasant smile.

"I just wanted to thank you for being so nice to her. I have been in and out of hospitals for over twenty years, and I know how important good nurses are."

Memories of some of the nurses I previously knew filled my mind. There was Maureen, who took time away from her busy schedule and spent hours brushing out my matted "bed-head." There was Julie, who graciously agreed to wash my grubby hair in the sink when doctors would not permit me to take a full shower. Then there was Teresa, who sat with me and laughed as we watched sitcoms when her shift was over.

These thoughts caused me to sob like a blubbering idiot to this young nurse. I gasped for air as I hugged her good-bye. With her arms around me, she patted me on the back and calmed me down. She must have thought to herself, "How did this howling nut case get out of the psych ward? Security?!"

*   *   *

When I began putting this book together, I considered leaving this story out. Essentially, this was because I was so embarrassed! As a survivor of a serious car crash, I do not like to admit I am often a <u>huge</u> crybaby!

However, this time I decided to just tough it out. Of course, I know how very important it is to have good doctors, surgeons and therapists. Yet, this message sings thanks and praise to all the excellent nurses out there who are often overlooked! Take it from someone who knows . . . when you are feeling crummy, a warm friendly smile is better than any drug. A good nurse can make all the difference.

On the way home, two men in dark business suits stood behind me. We waited for the streetlight to change. Their conversation suggested they were regional managers from the expensive lingerie shop *La Perla*.

"Ya see . . . it's all about the underwear . . . If a woman doesn't feel good when she wakes up, it can ruin her whole day!"

A syrupy smell floated through the air and teased my nose as we stood outside *Garrett Popcorn Shop.* The welcoming aroma reminded me of a grandmother's house! This, along with the overheard comments, made me think of sweet Rosie. How would she feel when her son arrived? The thoughtful nurse took care of her hair and makeup but what about the dull hospital gown? I knew I had to do something about it!

*   *   *

I went into the discount store around the corner. There, I bought her a cute nightgown covered in pink flowers by the designer Karen Neuburger. Although I had to guess the size, I was sure this low-priced gift was called for—maybe not by the doctor's mouth, but by the patient's heart! I learned from my nurses so many years before that inexpensive things can often be the most valuable.

TERRY

The patient I came to see walked slowly to the bathroom. He kept his head down as he slid slowly across the floor. The tan, fuzzy slippers given to him when he arrived covered his feet.

I introduced myself, and he looked up in a daze. He told me he would like to receive Communion but asked if I could come back in a few minutes. A boring and humdrum day was all that awaited me at home, so I gladly agreed. I decided to sit in the lounge.

Once there, I met a woman by the name of Terry who sat by herself. We talked, and I learned her daughter was a patient in the hospital and had just left her room for a series of tests. The mother did not offer any more information about her daughter's medical condition, so I did not pry.

Instead, I changed the topic of conversation from the patient to the mother herself. I began by complimenting Mom for being there. I assured her that her presence was important. Years before, many of my "hospital neighbors" did not have the strong support system of friends and family I always had. This often resulted in slower and less successful recoveries.

In addition, I could guarantee that although her daughter might not always express her gratitude right now, someday she would understand and be grateful for all her mother did. I knew this because of my own feelings. There were many days during my hospital stay when my frustration kept me from showing thanks to my own family.

*   *   *

Now I know that being there for someone you care about is a <u>gift</u>—that is why we call it "being <u>present</u>."

When I walked home, this point again became apparent to me. There had been a nasty snowstorm the night before. Although the streets and sidewalks were reasonably clear, during that time of year I often have a problem when I reach each corner. The city snowplows leave small piles of snow and slush at the end of each sidewalk. Most pedestrians simply hop over these little wet inconveniences. However, my poor balance leaves me unable to perform this necessary winter dance step. I must trudge through the mess. My clumsiness leaves me with damp socks and very cold feet!

That day, only about two blocks from home, I struggled through one of these trouble spots. I felt my right foot going as I lost my balance. I rushed to put my left down, only to have it land on more ice! Back to the right—slip—then to the left—slide! This went on and on as I flung my arms around and roared, "Whoa! Whoa! Wwwhhooaa!!" A "snowball effect" in winter—how fitting.

I kept looking down at the sidewalk, trying unsuccessfully to find dry land. Out of the corner of my eyes, I saw a dark image rushing toward me at full speed. My mind was busy worrying about keeping myself upright. Therefore, my head stayed down and I ignored the figure.

That is, until I felt him grab my arm. I heard, "You're alright—just take it slow!"

He was the homeless man who stood outside the Dunkin' Donuts shop on the next corner. I did not know much about him, only that he was usually there when I walked to or from the hospital. Our conversations were always brief and included friendly smiles and straightforward well wishes. Yet, that day this "unknown friend" proved to be my hero.

The next day I sat in the hallway and saw a young man walk by. He looked to be in his mid-thirties. With his head down, he pulled a pole on wheels that held his I.V. bag. Even in the ragged hospital gown, he looked handsome and his strong build hinted he was once a star football player! I guessed he had broken many girls' hearts—as the thought of him there alone broke mine.

The slow laps he did around the hospital floor had to be dull and boring. Yet, they seemed his desperate attempt to find some sort of entertainment. In the silence of the hallway, his expression screamed, "I hate it here! I'm so fed up! I want to leave!"

*　　*　　*

He passed me three or four times. I knew it was my turn to be "a present" . . . so I called him over for a chat.

UDANT

"There's my girlfriend!" I heard as I walked into the room.

The patient in this bed was an elderly man with smiling eyes and a sweet grin that could melt anyone's heart. Although I had met him only two days before, he already labeled me with this honorable title! I was flattered.

We talked for a few minutes. Due to throat problems, his voice was raspy and hoarse. This made it difficult to understand him, as I am sure my slurred speech made it tricky for him to understand me! Fortunately, we conquered these speech problems and filled our days together with good-humored jokes and many laughs.

While there that day, an intern came in to speak with Udant. I stepped back to the window, sat on the couch and gave them some privacy. I did not know much about Udant or his medical condition. However, I heard a few expressions from the intern such as, "You'll heal faster this time . . ." and "It's too bad this happened . . ." and "We didn't expect it . . ."

When the intern left I returned to Udant's bedside. He lay there and his eyes stared down at the clean white sheets. It was if he searched for answers in the midst of the bedding's blankness. However, the absence of color only represented his inability to understand what he felt.

"Yikes! What happened?" I asked. His teary eyes refused to look at me. He pressed his lips together and shook his head.

"They just won't admit they've made a mistake . . . I admit it whenever **I** do something wrong," he said quietly as he tried to hold back his tears.

Rubbing his arm, I told him about the many times I have felt the same frustration. Without thinking, I then made an unoriginal remark that gets overused: "We all make mistakes."

Yeah . . . I'm sure that made him feel better.

Now as I sit here at my computer I realize, "We all <u>have</u> to make mistakes." After all, there is no up without a down, no morning without a night, no good without a bad, and no accomplishments without mistakes. Mistakes can often be painful and are never very easy, but we can always overcome them with our faith.

Recently, I have learned the Indian name "Udant" means "correct message." However, I doubt he really <u>wanted</u> to hear the truth at that particular time. None of us ever <u>want</u> to hear a world leader, a courtroom judge or a medical doctor admit, "Oops, I have made a mistake!" (regardless of their accuracy!)

My own example of this is when I had a bone marrow biopsy. After the excruciatingly painful procedure, I waited on the table. Then, I heard one technician say to the other, "Mike, we have a problem." Her serious tone reminded me of the famous line used by the Apollo 13 crew back in 1970 to report a technical fault in the oxygen tanks ("Houston, we have a problem . . .").

This time, the message concluded with the announcement, "I've dropped the piece and lost it on the floor." That was definitely something I did not want to hear! Nor did I need to. Tears ran down my face, and I was sure I was about to vomit! All I could think was, "Honey, you better find it . . . 'cause you ain't goin' back in there!" I lay silent—paralyzed with fear as I thought about how painful a repeat experience would be!

*   *   *

Fortunately, they soon found what they lost. Despite this happy ending, I would have preferred to learn about the mishap after the procedure was over! For the rest of my time there, I questioned their competence and misread every ache and pain. If Udant had heard the "correct message" sooner, anger might have taken over and clouded his vision as he looked ahead. This might have lead to poor decisions.

*　　*　　*

Before I left his bedside, Udant wiped his eyes. They held tears his proud emotions prevented from falling. Quietly, he apologized for crying.

"Oh, you never have to express any regret for crying . . . you and I have earned the right to cry!" An old friend told me something he once heard at an Alcoholics Anonymous meeting: "When we cry, God cries, too." After all, no father likes to see his own child in pain!

I turned to walk out of the room and added firmly, "And don't you ever believe you are weak for doing so! It takes a lot of very strong emotions to cry, and anyone who feels them is certainly not weak!"

NATHAN

Before I started my visits for the day, I talked with a Catholic chaplain who sat at the other desk in the office. He was a tall, thin and very striking man with big bright eyes and a charming British accent. He was undoubtedly the type of man Shakespeare had in mind when he introduced us to Romeo!

"The people in this country move much too fast," he pointed out to me. "It always seems like they are in such a hurry to get somewhere! Where are they going? Why do they always feel they have to rush and get things done quickly?"

I walked into a room later that morning and found a man lying helplessly in his hospital bed. A shiny, white, very hard, plastic brace held him still. Its bright color reminded me of "Romeo's" eyes. Fred Astaire danced across the television set hanging on the wall in front of him. However, it was obvious that Nathan did not see the program. A blank stare with glassy eyes made it apparent he was in deep thought.

After I approached the bed, I introduced myself and told him why I had come. My words startled him and brought him back into the "real world." However, his saddened look indicated he was not yet sure all of this was "real."

Then, I became aware of a woman who sat quietly in the corner reading a book. With a pleasant smile, she introduced herself as Nathan's wife, Rachel. She told me Nathan's injures were from a high-speed motorcycle accident. Ironically, this information reminded me of "Romeo's" observation.

She went on to tell me how difficult this was for their children. It was hard for them to see their father in such a vulnerable position, she explained. In the past, he was always seen as the pillar of strength in the household—always there to protect them from any danger. Yet, the crash made it apparent that everyone is susceptible to harm—even our superheroes. Evidently, Nathan was not the only victim in this accident. His family also suffered.

What is more, I realized he probably blamed himself for their pain. I remembered the guilt I felt when I looked into my family members' concerned eyes as they stared down at me in my hospital bed. Pain is often harder to watch than to experience.

He rested quietly in his bed while his wife talked for a few more minutes. When he heard himself described as "vulnerable," I noticed his eyes filled with tears. The idea of being weak and open to danger was difficult for him to grasp, too.

*   *   *

Walking home that afternoon from the hospital, I thought about this visit. Nathan clearly took good care of his health. For this reason, I was convinced recovery was a very good bet.

However, the fact that everyone will experience some type of serious illness or injury is something we all must remember. In addition, I suppose it was beneficial for his children to see him in that condition. Once the broken pillar healed, they would better understand and appreciate his strength.

A few weeks later, I thought I recognized Nathan's name once again on the patient list. This worried me. I had learned from doctors that injuries like those caused in Nathan's accident frequently do not show their ugly faces until long after the initial incident. Concerned his health had taken a turn for the worst, I hurried to the room to find out if he was back.

Boy, was I wrong! Yes, this was the same man, but I am not sure I would have known him unless I saw Rachel on the couch next to him. This new, well-built, very attractive man now sat upright in a chair wearing a much less confining back brace. He looked at me as I walked in. His big smile and bright eyes told me he remembered who I was.

*   *   *

I found out this visit was for another back surgery. Learning he had returned reminded me that once a pillar breaks, the expectation of a complete recovery is impractical. However, seeing him and hearing all he had achieved reminded me that broken does not always mean worse—maybe just a little bit different!

IRVING

My long morning of patient visits would soon be finished. I knew my husband would be home from work soon for his lunch break. An apartment full of dusty furniture, with a pile of dirty laundry and a dishwasher packed with dishes, awaited me at home. Anxious to finish up and get to it all, I hurried into my last room.

Irving lay quietly in his bed. The bright rays from the morning sun outlined his figure. This made him look almost spiritual. I expected to hear a gospel choir accompanied by harps as I entered the room! The old paperback prayer book in his hands looked worn out and over read.

He looked up at me and grinned. His eyes gave off a welcoming sparkle. This, along with his round face and gray hair, reminded me of a clean shaven Santa Claus! I quickly forgot about my wifely duties at home.

We began talking, and I told him a story about my young niece, Katie. One day, my husband and I were visiting my parents. My younger sister and her family were also there. We all went to Mass at Mom and Dad's church. Dad stepped up to the altar to help administer Communion. When the priest handed Dad the big gold chalice, Katie became excited and yelled in a loud whisper, "Papa won the trophy! Papa won the trophy!" The quiet audience sitting around us laughed at her entertaining cry!

"Now it's time for you to get the prize!" I told the patient. I said a prayer and did my business. After giving him the spiritual host, I turned to walk out. When I was almost at the doorway, he called me back and told me he wanted to give *me* something.

Unsure of what this could be, I returned to his bedside. Any gift from Santa was bound to be a good one, right?

He then told me that he was a retired priest and he wanted to give me a blessing! I threw my head back and laughed. "Oh, no!" I exclaimed. I felt like I had just learned Mozart was in the room while I was playing the piano! "Well, how did I do?"

He chuckled and told me I did fine. Then he reached up to my forehead, made the sign of the cross with his thumb, and said a simple prayer.

I sat in the chair next to his bed, and we talked about our shared belief that God is a giver—not a taker. He said, "Based on this idea, patients often pray for the wrong thing. Taking the pain away is not something we should ask of God. Instead, we should pray to Him to give us strength to endure whatever we must face."

His doctors were discussing what their next step would be to aid his aging heart. They were trying to decide whether they could just put a stent in or if he needed open heart surgery. Then, he said something I found surprising to come from a man of such strong faith,

"Ya know, I would just rather die. I'm too old for this. I don't want to go through surgery."

"WHAT DO YOU MEAN!? You're a priest!" I reminded him. "You shouldn't be saying stuff like that! You're supposed to always encourage people to live."

* * *

"Oh, you know what I mean, Laur. It's the quality of life that matters, not the quantity."

I gave him a sympathetic smile and a pat on his leg to let him know I understood. Then, I got up to leave and added, "In that case, I guess you should also pray for your doctors and nurses. We both know that no matter whom you are or what the circumstances are, prayer always provides valuable guidance and support!"

As I walked out, he complimented me by saying, "Ya know, Laur, meeting you has really been the best thing that's happened to me since I got here!"

"Thanks, Father. But that's really not saying much . . . you <u>are</u> in a hospital."

TINA

I sat in the office early one Monday morning and enjoyed a muffin and cup of hot tea I bought on the way there from the espresso bar at Nordstrom's. I looked over the patient list and noticed a female patient who was only eighteen years old. Although not assigned to her floor, I considered visiting her. After all, I certainly knew how scary it was to be in a hospital at any age. Most of the volunteers were at least forty years older than she was. I thought my younger age might comfort her.

However, her age was the exact same reason I was reluctant to go. Like her, my injuries occurred when I was only eighteen. I was worried her situation was a little "too close to home," and I was not quite sure I could handle it.

After debating about it myself, I decided not to go. A chaplain walked into the office just as I was about to leave.

"Oh, Laura! There is a family up in Room 1472. They would like to receive Communion. If you have time, could you stop there?"

Right away, I guessed what her answer would be, but I asked anyway, "Is that the girl who is eighteen?" Sure enough, it was. "Well," I figured, "God must want me to go there." So, I took a few deep breaths and was on my way up to the fourteenth floor.

Tina lay completely still. Three or four people stood around her bed with tears in their eyes. No one said a word.

I started talking to them and found them to be her family. Her mother told me a bizarre and unexpected mishap during cheerleading practice resulted in Tina's neck being broken. This energetic, young teenager, who once sat at the top of the pyramid, now lay motionless.

Tina kept her lips pressed firmly together. She listened to and definitely understood everything Mom said. Occasionally, Tina rolled her sweet baby blue eyes in disgust at the remarks. "I think it's all finally hitting her . . . what has happened and what it all means," her mother explained.

I thought to myself, "Maybe it's the first time, but it won't be the last . . . and it will hurt just as much (if not more) every time." Giving her a gentle smile, I told Tina, "Just remember . . . there is no such thing as a forever pain—pain always goes away. It might take medicine, an operation, therapy or whatever, but when things get tough, just remind yourself, 'Somehow, every kind of pain always goes away.'"

She looked at me and gave me half a smile plus a weak thumbs-up sign. I thought this was her way of telling me, "Enough with the motivational speeches! I've heard them all!" Sadly, this type of message seemed inappropriate, as it came through the eyes of a cheerleader.

I knew she had a long and difficult road ahead of her. Getting her hint, I said, "Good bye!" and left her room.

* * *

Sorrow, fear and anger take up a lot of time and energy. To be successful in rehab (or life!), a person cannot afford to limit either. Tina had to let these feelings go. In hard times, people spend too much time crying about what they lost instead of being thankful for what they still hold.

I think people often mix up the words "forgive" and "forget." In my case, I cannot do the drunk driver the favor of **forgetting** what happened . . . just look at me! I hear the crash every time I slur a sentence, I see it every time my weak hand tries to write a word, and I feel it every time I take a step.

However, I must do myself the favor of **forgiving** him. The word "forgive" is all about <u>you</u>. This verb forcefully gives you orders. The first part, "<u>for</u>," means "directed to" or "aimed at," and the latter, "<u>give</u>," means "to assign" or "hand over." Clearly, this word is a double whammy way of telling you to get rid of something!

Although I was sure Tina would probably reach this point of forgiveness, I also knew a few other things. I knew the unfortunate truth that in all likelihood Tina would spend a long time in a wheelchair that was much too big for her. I knew the humiliation she would feel when her date had to cut her meat at a restaurant. I knew the heartache she would go through when she was unable to dance to the loud music at a party. And I knew the insignificance she would feel when she went out with friends months from now and heard them tell stories about the fun times they had without her. I knew because some things my mind can't forget.

However, I knew even more! I knew the laughter this young girl would enjoy as she sped down the hallways in her wheelchair, racing other patients her age. I knew the satisfaction she would sense after she completed basic tasks like buttoning her jacket. I knew how valuable common things would become after she almost lost them. And I knew of the significant number of new friends she would make who clearly understood all she went through. I knew because some things my heart won't forget.

On the walk home, the sky was gray and it looked like rain. I passed my friend in front of the Dunkin' Donuts. He waited to collect any change customers still held in their hands.

"Hey . . . what's going on here? Get that sunshine out of your pocket!" I ordered as I laughed. "I know you're hiding it!"

He chuckled and said, "I wish I could, Laur! I sure wish I could just pull it out of my pocket!"

"Well . . . you're the one in charge of the weather!"

He looked down, raised one eyebrow and rubbed his chin as he thought for a moment. Then he promised, "Okay . . . tomorrow it will be here!"

Sure enough, the next morning I walked to the hospital under a bright, blue sky! I passed my friend and said, "I don't know how you did it, but thank you!"

* * *

I hope Tina always remembers to check her pockets.

YOU

Recently, I read an article about Mother Teresa of Calcutta. It revealed that many times during her life this very inspirational woman questioned her own faith and connection to God. She prayed to Him to help her regain it. I found this to be interesting as well as quite comforting. After a car crash almost killed me, any questions I had about my religion and my God seemed more understandable and acceptable. I figured if someone like Mother Teresa had uncertainties about her beliefs, why couldn't I?

Coincidently, a few days later I heard a priest discuss the idea that we are not born with faith—it is a gift from God. I thought to myself, "Well, I guess if God doesn't want to give it to you, you are just out of luck!" Fortunately, I then remembered the piece I read about Mother Teresa and what she often felt she had to do.

Occasionally, when I am talking to patients or family members, I tell them what I learned from this article. They thank me and tell me they thought they were alone in their feelings.

* * *

I wrote this book as **MY OPPORTUNITY** to assure you that many have felt and are still feeling what you are experiencing. Please know that whether your tragedy is physical, emotional or whatever, you are never alone.

"Do not fear, for I am with you;
Do not be afraid, for I am your God;
I will strengthen you,
I will help you,
I will uphold you with my victorious right
hand"

Isaiah 41:10

NOTES

NOTES

NOTES

NOTES

NOTES

NOTES